Dinosaur Detectives
Search for the facts...

Moschops
and Other
Ancient Reptiles

Tracey Kelly

raintree
a Capstone company — publishers for children

Raintree is an imprint of Capstone Global Library Limited, a company incorporated in England and Wales having its registered office at 264 Banbury Road, Oxford, OX2 7DY – Registered company number: 6695582

www.raintree.co.uk
myorders@raintree.co.uk

© Brown Bear Books Limited 2018
This edition published by Raintree in 2020.
The moral rights of the proprietor have been asserted.

Text: Tracey Kelly
Designer: John Woolford
Design Manager: Keith Davis
Editorial Director: Lindsey Lowe
Children's Publisher: Anne O'Daly
Picture Manager: Sophie Mortimer
Production by Katy LaVigne
Printed and bound in India

ISBN 978 1 4747 7829 9 (hardback)
ISBN 978 1 4747 7835 0 (paperback)

British Library Cataloguing in Publication Data
A full catalogue record for this book is available from the British Library.

Acknowledgements
We would like to thank the following for permission to reproduce photographs:
Public Domain: Granger 4.

Every effort has been made to contact copyright holders of material reproduced in this book. Any omissions will be rectified in subsequent printings if notice is given to the publisher.

All the internet addresses (URLs) given in this book were valid at the time of going to press. However, due to the dynamic nature of the internet, some addresses may have changed, or sites may have changed or ceased to exist since publication. While the author and publisher regret any inconvenience this may cause readers, no responsibility for any such changes can be accepted by either the author or the publisher.

Contents

How do we know about dinosaurs?

Scientists are like detectives.

They look at fossils.

Fossils tell us where dinosaurs and other ancient reptiles lived.

They tell us how big they were.

Robert Broom was a dinosaur detective. He found *Moschops* fossils in 1910. He found them in South Africa. *Moschops* had a thick skull. People guessed that it used its head to fight.

How to use this book

This tells you what the animal ate.

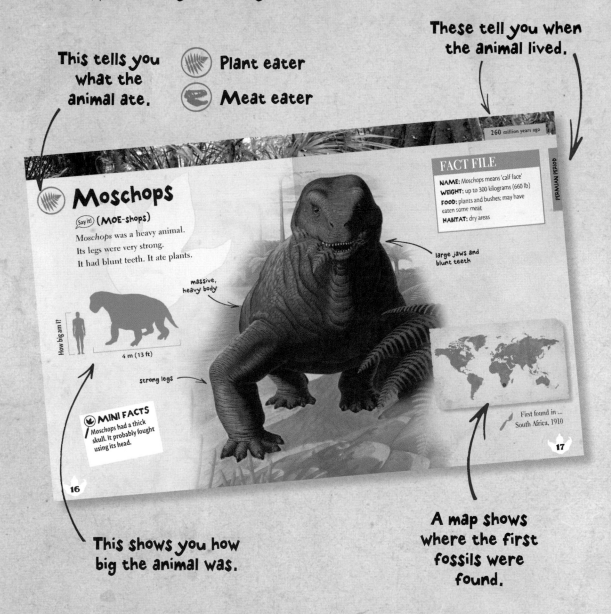

Plant eater

Meat eater

These tell you when the animal lived.

260 million years ago

PERMIAN PERIOD

Moschops

Say it! (MOE-shops)

Moschops was a heavy animal.
Its legs were very strong.
It had blunt teeth. It ate plants.

How big am I?

4 m (13 ft)

massive, heavy body

strong legs

MINI FACTS
Moschops had a thick skull. It probably fought using its head.

16

FACT FILE

NAME: Moschops means 'calf face'
WEIGHT: up to 300 kilograms (660 lb)
FOOD: plants and bushes; may have eaten some meat
HABITAT: dry areas

large jaws and blunt teeth

First found in ...
South Africa, 1910

17

This shows you how big the animal was.

A map shows where the first fossils were found.

Read on to become a dinosaur detective!

What was Earth like?

Moschops lived in the Permian period.
That was millions of years ago.
Earth was very dry. Plants grew near water
pools. Ancient reptiles ate and drank there.

Bradysaurus

Say it! (BRAY-dee-SAW-rus)

Bradysaurus had a huge body.
It had strong limbs. Its head had bony
ridges. Its teeth were shaped like leaves.

head 'crown' made of
bony ridges

MINI FACTS

Bradysaurus moved
slowly. It was clumsy!
The turtle might be
related to it!

PERMIAN PERIOD

FACT FILE

NAME: *Bradysaurus* means 'Brady's lizard' or 'slow reptile'

WEIGHT: up to 1 tonne (1 ton)

FOOD: plants

HABITAT: large swamps

How big am I?

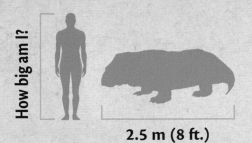

2.5 m (8 ft.)

big body

hard scales

short, strong limbs

First found in ...
South Africa, 1914

Coelurosauravus

 Say it! (SEEL-your-oh-SAW-rave-us)

Coelurosauravus looked like a lizard with wings! Each wing had 22 tiny bones. These were covered with skin. *Coelurosauravus* could glide in the air.

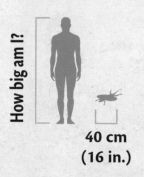

How big am I?

40 cm
(16 in.)

long head with frill

🦖 **MINI FACTS**

Coelurosauravus was the first animal that could glide.

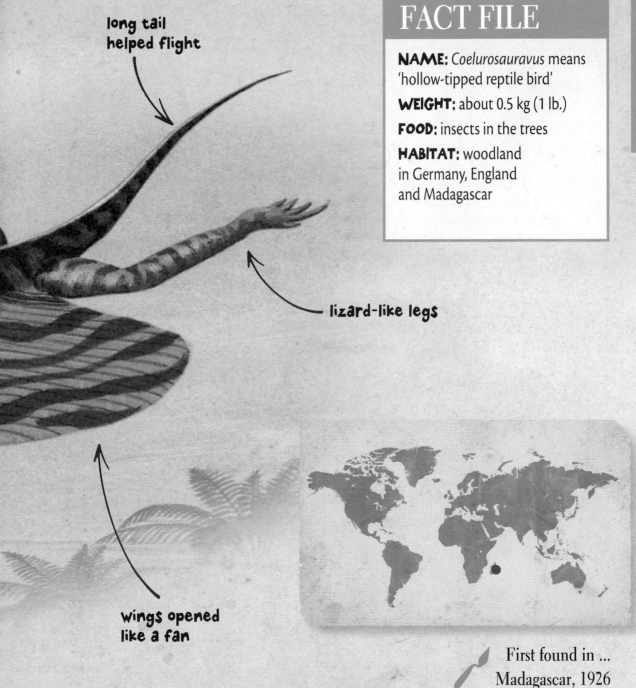

long tail
helped flight

FACT FILE

NAME: *Coelurosauravus* means 'hollow-tipped reptile bird'

WEIGHT: about 0.5 kg (1 lb.)

FOOD: insects in the trees

HABITAT: woodland in Germany, England and Madagascar

lizard-like legs

wings opened
like a fan

First found in ...
Madagascar, 1926

Dicynodon

Say it! (dye-SINE-oh-don)

Dicynodon had a bulky body, a bit like a pig. It had strong legs. Its large teeth could break off plants.

horny beak, used to bite plants

FACT FILE

NAME: *Dicynodon* means 'two dog-teeth'
WEIGHT: 11 kg (24 lbs.)
FOOD: plants and roots
HABITAT: most lived on land, but a few lived in the water

How big am I?

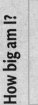

1.2 m (4 ft.)

MINI FACTS

Dicynodon lived in groups. This kept it safe from meat eaters.

pig-like body shape

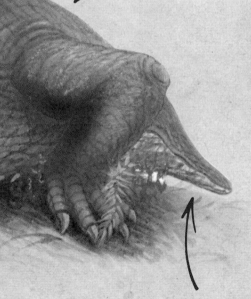

short tail

First found in ...
South Africa, 1845

13

Dimetrodon

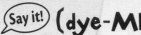 (dye-MEE-troe-don)

Dimetrodon had a huge head.

It had a 'sail' of skin on its back.

The sail soaked up the sun's heat.

sharp teeth for cutting meat

MINI FACTS

Dimetrodon had long teeth for tearing flesh. It had short teeth for chewing.

skin like a crocodile's

How big am I?

3.5 m (11 ft.)

sail of skin

FACT FILE

NAME: *Dimetrodon* means 'two measures of teeth'

WEIGHT: 250 kg (550 lbs.)

FOOD: animals and insects

HABITAT: swamps of the southwestern United States, Canada, Russia and Eastern Europe

First found in ...
Texas and Oklahoma,
United States, 1870s

legs spread out
to the sides

15

Moschops

Say it! (MOE-shops)

Moschops was a heavy animal.
Its legs were very strong.
It had blunt teeth. It ate plants.

massive, heavy body

How big am I?

4 m (13 ft.)

strong legs

🔍 **MINI FACTS**

Moschops had a thick skull. It probably fought using its head.

FACT FILE

NAME: *Moschops* means 'calf face'

WEIGHT: up to 300 kg (660 lbs.)

FOOD: plants and bushes; may have eaten some meat

HABITAT: dry areas

large jaws and
blunt teeth

First found in ...
South Africa, 1910

17

Lystrosaurus

(Say it!) (LISS-tro-SAW-russ)

Lystrosaurus had wide feet.

They helped it walk on swampy ground.

Some reptiles lived in the Triassic period.

 MINI FACTS

Lystrosaurus probably lived in or near water.
It lived in herds.
That kept it safe.

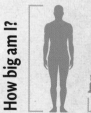

How big am I?

1 m (3 ft.)

tusks, used to tear plants

FACT FILE

NAME: *Lystrosaurus* means 'shovel lizard'
WEIGHT: 91 kg (200 lbs.)
FOOD: water plants
HABITAT: near swamps, lakes and coasts around the world

heavy, barrel-
shaped body

short,
stubby tail

First found in ...
South Africa, 1867

Euparkeria

 Say it! (YOU-park-EAR-ree-ah)

Euparkeria had a tiny body.

It had long back legs.

It ran fast to hunt prey.

How big am I?

60 cm (2 ft.)

 MINI FACTS

Euparkeria could run very fast. It could probably run across water and not fall in!

sharp teeth, used
to kill prey

long tail, used
for balance

FACT FILE

NAME: *Euparkeria* means 'Parker's reptile'
WEIGHT: up to 4.5 kg (10 lbs.)
FOOD: smaller animals
HABITAT: forest floors in the
woodlands of South Africa

First found in ...
South Africa, 1913

ran on two legs

Dinosaur quiz

Test your dinosaur detective skills!
Can you answer these questions?
Look in the book for clues.
The answers are on page 24.

1 What kind of teeth did *Bradysaurus* have? What did it eat?

2 Which dinosaur lived near swamps, lakes and coasts?

3 Why did *Dimetrodon* have a sail on its back?

4 Was *Euparkeria* a fast or slow runner?

22

Glossary

fossil
Part of an animal or plant in rock.
The animal or plant lived in ancient times.

habitat
The kind of place where an animal usually lives.

herd
A group of animals that lives together.

meat eater
An animal that eats mostly meat.

plant eater
An animal that eats only plants.

prey
An animal that is hunted
by other animals for food.

Triassic period
The time that
came after the
Permian period.

Find out more

Books

National Geographic Little Kids
First Big Book of Dinosaurs, Catherine
D. Hughes (National Geographic Kids,
2011)

The Big Book of Dinosaurs,
DK Editors (DK Children, 2015)

Websites

www.bbc.co.uk/sn/prehistoric_life/
dinosaurs

www.natgeokids.com/uk/play-and-
win/games/dinosaur-memory

www.nhm.ac.uk/discover/dino-
directory

Index

Quiz answers: 1. *Bradysaurus* had leaf-shaped teeth. It ate plants. **2.** *Lystrosaurus.* **3.** The sail
helped *Dimetrodon* to soak up heat from the sun. **4.** It was a fast runner.